I0087117

BOSSHION

A PERSONAL NOTE AND MENTAL STYLE GUIDE FOR TODAYS LEADING #BOSSBABE

DEBORAH HARRIS

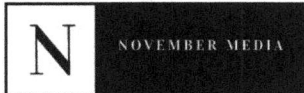

N NOVEMBER MEDIA
PUBLISHING & CONSULTING FIRM

Deborah Harris

November Media Publishing, Chicago IL.

Copyright © 2016 Deborah Harris

All rights reserved. No part of this publication may be reproduced, distributed, or transmitted in any form or by any means, including photocopying, recording, or other electronic or mechanical methods, without the prior written permission of the publisher, except in the case of brief quotations embodied in critical reviews and certain other noncommercial uses permitted by copyright law. For permission requests, write to the publisher, addressed "Attention: Permissions Coordinator," at the email address below. November Media novmedia10@gmail.com

Ordering Information: Special discounts are available on quantity purchases by corporations, associations, and others. For details, contact the publisher at the email address above.

Printed in the United States of America

ISBN: 0692761799 ISBN-13: 978-0692761793

Cover Design: T Jones Media
Interior Design: November Media Publishing
Editing: Candice Jackson

I **dedicate** this to my heavenly Father who never gave up on me... To all the women before me who looked adversity directly in the eye without flinching... I found my voice because of YOU! Thank you Tiheasha... I'm so ready and so grateful to November Media Publishing... let's have some fun girl.

TABLE OF CONTENTS

OPENING NOTE

I am strong, I am brave, I am tender, I am fierce, I am crazy and wild...I am a force like none other.

The sheer truth of that statement came to me recently while I sat alone in my home. During this quiet time, I began to take stock of my life while writing in my favorite journal. I tend to do this every six months, but this time around something was different.

As I reminisced over the past several years, my memory ran into a few old friends name depression and self-pity. I'm sure I'm not the only woman that has battled or is currently battling with emotions such as this. So trust me when I say that you're not alone.

Initially, my first thought when faced with these old emotions or beliefs of myself was to look away and run because I didn't want to think about how dark of a place I had been in for so long. I didn't want to think about how I felt that no one wanted me or believed in me and the aspirations that I had for my life. I soon found myself wanting to pick and choose which memories to keep so that the overall picture became more attractive.

In nearly an instant, my heart stopped my mind and forced me to see what had been lingering all those years amongst the depression and self-pity: courage and fight. For so long, I could only focus on the negative and was blinded to the fact that I never ever gave up on what woke me up every morning and what I dreamt about every night: to help change lives.

The whole experience felt like a double out of body moment in time. I was able to see what God sees when He looks at how far I've come. I was able to see how I picked myself up after every failed class and semesters missed because of a severe illness in college. I was able to see how resilient I stood after meeting the entire biology department and hearing them tell me I should change majors because I wasn't cut out for this field. I was able to feel the smile on my heart as I walked across the stage after winning the battle. I was able to understand my purpose in moving to another city that I believed held no future for me. I was able to see myself cry over and over again for years and still drag myself out of bed while searching for a reason to move forward and not end my life. Most importantly, I was able to realize that I had grabbed hold of my truth somewhere along the way.

This truth woke me up to who I am and what I chased in life. I seek to find truth and beauty in everything I see and place my hand to. This particular way of living is not always the easiest because seeing truth and beauty through the mud, tears, broken promises, and shortcomings can sometimes cloud even the clearest of days. Standing firm upon who you are at the very heart of you, is what births greatness, it's what eases the pain of some sacrifices, it's what causes mountains to move for you, it's what creates leaders and great influencers of our time and times past.

This truth freed me to love all of me and rejoice within myself. People took notice in the most interesting ways because my approach to life was my own, and I didn't seek outside approval any longer. I began to let go of everyone else's standard for my life and be content and grateful for where I was. I began to believe that I had strength and savvy within me in order to get to my desired destination.

This new way of living and thinking allowed me shine from the inside out, and I began to see the difference it was making in my interactions. There have been people I've met along my winding journey who believed me to be a major fashion blogger, assembly woman, owner of a successful business, owner of land, and even a happily married mother of three. It became apparent to me that not only are these serious goals of some form for my life, but I was already walking in it and had no idea.

For me, this is the most important key to becoming your own leader: Living in outstanding excellence at every point in your life.

PROLOGUE

Our clothes and style say a lot about who we are, where we are from, and sometimes even our occupation. For women especially, our clothing throughout the centuries has played a major role in shaping and remembering the history of kingdoms and social movements alike. When we research history revolving around the Elizabethan eras, we are mesmerized by the surface depictions of leaders and their lifestyles. What resonates even louder than the fabulous apparel and jewelry that adorned such women was their outspoken heart and mind when approaching the well-being of humanity.

Have you ever thought to yourself what such iconic

figures with great fashion sense have in common? Although outwardly we see the clothing and jewels that adorn them, their glorious nature has nothing to do with what the person was physically wearing necessarily and their style has nothing to do with how the individuals put it all together.

When we study women of the Elizabethan era, the Dior woman that spawned forth after World War II, and some of today's high profile leading ladies, we notice the common threads of power, boldness, femininity, and grace. These traits have been the pillars or foundations that have created some of the most envied women of past and present time.

Most of you I'm sure have heard the saying that goes something like, "The clothes don't make the lady, the lady makes the clothes." In my opinion, truer words could not have been spoken when it comes to deciphering what all powerful women throughout the ages have in common: Great Bosshion Sense.

Well at this point you may begin to ask yourself; what is or defines Bosshion Sense?

Bosshion Sense is related to a general savvy and know-how that most people feel are ingrained traits from birth, but it goes a step further because this particular sense of self is both within us and developed over time through trial and error. It is my firm belief that leaders are developed in the fire and like my grandmother always said, "You have to pay the cost to be the BOSS."

In our world today, we see plenty of emphasis being placed on the power of a "Girl Boss" and how "Boss Babes" around the world are influencing this generation and new levels of entrepreneurship and philanthropy.

What I noticed being highlighted from a surface perspective, are the styles in which these ladies dress and the access to luxury living. When we examine women like Michelle Obama, Shonda Rhimes, Oprah Winfrey, Bob Bland and our mothers as well, we wonder how these ladies get up and run the world with effortless style and grace every day. How do these women manage to look and speak flawlessly approximately 100% of the time in the public eye?

While the glitz and glamour of their position is appealing, we must look at the mental and spiritual makeup of our respected leading ladies. What inward qualities hold the secret to their success which then makes people and opportunities gravitate toward them?

I'm sorry to have to dethrone the myth that it's their Maybelline or top of the line stylist. The truth is that these ladies possess fundamental "Boss" factors.

These particular "Boss" factors we will discuss, are traits that make everything these women say, do, and wear come alive and demand attention and respect. The truth of the matter is that you can't merely dress like a boss, you have to KNOW you're one from the inside out.

When a woman knows who she is internally and understands that a BOSS state of mind is her most valuable accessory, everything about her moves in the direction she seeks and the universe responds accordingly.

Here, we will uncover the elements and sometimes harsh truths behind good Bosshion Sense and how to style our inner selves with a few fundamental accessories.

"There is nothing wrong with your body, but there is a lot wrong with the messages which try to convince you otherwise."

—Rae Smith

Deborah Harris

CHAPTER ONE
Love the Skin You're In

One of the most important choices of covering for a leading lady is her skin…naturally. Being confident in what God gave you from birth is a bold statement maker all on its own, and every top lady boss in the world knows this secret. I like to think of your skin as the starter point to building a great outfit. Taking care of your outer shell is the responsibility of no one except for yourself, and this process is done from the inside out. Having a balanced routine for the inner and outer maintenance of your temple, adds to the release and intake of positive energy as well as interactions with yourself and others.

When I speak of interactions with yourself, I'm referring to how you feel and think about your identity and becoming in tune with your soul and thoughts concerning yourself. Find out how to look yourself in the mirror daily and speak life and love over your temple. Speaking to yourself is a great discipline and will come naturally as you begin to become those words you are placing into the universe. We have to remember that our bodies respond to what we feed it, and that doesn't stop at what we physically place in our mouths but rather begins with what we allow to come out of it.

A verse within the bible that I particularly love is from Psalm 139:14 and it reads, "I praise you because I am fearfully and wonderfully made; your works are wonderful, I know that full well." Repeating this daily and especially in the face of moments that try to shave away your self-esteem, will access a realm of enlightenment to the beauty and complexity of your true self.

Your true self is essentially the most naked and bare parts about you and consequently, these are also the parts we like to hide. I've noticed this particular action with myself when I was younger and other women that I have mentored over the years. It amazes me how women have a tendency both consciously and subconsciously to place on the skin of others. Women are masters of multiple personalities and masks, and we often times covet the lives of other women. The scary thing about this practice is that we begin to layer so many traits and attributes of who we think we should be and who others are, that we lose any real connection to ourselves. We must not fear looking ourselves in the mirror with honesty because each and every one of us holds a specific measure of truth and love that this world needs to guide itself in the right direction.

What I love most about what is happening in today's society are the many voices that are speaking out particularly on the importance of body acceptance. This of course is extremely important because too many negative associations have been made concerning body image; not being able to accept and be proud of what you see in the mirror leads to psychological and physical traumas. This shift in body acceptance is being seen in one of the most influential industries in the world; the modeling industry. It's encouraging to have not only current super models but designers as well that demand more of a healthy frame for runway and commercial print. It's perceived that the light bulb went off for everyone at the same time concerning physical health, mental health, and acceptance. Beautiful moments have taken place on and off the runway because of this.

When a woman has embraced her heritage, race, culture, height, weight, and all the other intricacies of her being, there is a freedom born within her that people can feel and see from miles away. Every freckle, dimple, scar, birthmark, and stretch of skin tells a unique story of courage, survival, gentleness and times of reckless abandonment. I encourage you to have pride and own every detail that's staring back and challenging you to push forward without apology.

Loving how you were originally formed is where the fun begins and the build out becomes the most original and adventurous. Accessories such as jewels, jackets, stilettos, or shades of lipstick can't compete with the brilliant glow that comes bursting from your inner closet, although they are important on multiple levels.

Reflection

This piece of knowledge took me years to learn and I know many of you can relate.

Growing up as the ugly duckling was torture for me. My nickname was Miss Piggy, and boy did I hate it. Kids at school and even family members called me this because my nose was extremely large for my face and I was chubby when I was younger. I felt ugly of course and envious of my cousins and girls in my classroom that had petite noses and smaller frames.

The summer after my eighth grade graduation, my mother made me the cutest two piece striped short set, and my eldest cousins helped do my hair in one of the most popular 90's style at the time. When I looked in the mirror, my heart was split in half because a part of me saw a beautiful girl and the other part of me felt like it wasn't enough.

I'm guessing my cousin saw how uncomfortable I was and asked what was wrong. I answered that people called me Miss Piggy and that I wished boys at school looked at me like they did my other classmates. She laughed and began to explain that I was looking at things all wrong because Miss Piggy is Fabulous, rich, has a great guy and is her own Boss. Hearing those words made me feel a tad bit more at ease with myself because I never looked at it from that perspective.

I'm not saying that I had an entire 180-degree heart change after that day. No one turns it all around in one day.

In my late teens and early twenties, I was considered what my grandfather referred to as "A hopeless case." I can laugh about that now because for the most part I knew he was only poking fun, but on many levels, that simple phrase hit home. I had no idea who I was or where I wanted to go for that matter and he could tell.

My sense of self was lost in what people (like my parents) and friends expected me to be. I walked through a good portion of my life as a zombie and wearing the skin of other people because I thought being myself wasn't good enough for me or anyone else.

Looking back now, I remember the first moment I ever took a good hard look at myself and believed in my heart that I was beautiful and someone special without anyone having to convince me. It was around the time I had ended my junior season in track and field, and I needed to go shopping because I had lost a substantial amount of weight. My grandmother was the only one available to take me shopping and she enjoyed the experience more than I thought she would. We roamed into this retail chain called Dots, and she had picked out some outfits for me that I never would have chosen on my own because I was still uncomfortable with my body even though I looked smaller.

The first outfit I tried on was a nude color with flowers and came with a top and a skirt. When I walked out of the dressing room my grandmother's exact words were, "Ooooh now that's cute". When I looked in the mirror, I started picking out all of my body flaws from my arms being too big to the rolls on my back. I couldn't see what she saw completely, and I began to question her choice for this particular set of clothing. My grandmother said something to me so profound at that moment and so very simple that I still apply it and share this golden nugget with other young women as well.

Her exact words were "You got to know that you're the cutest thing walking around. I can't make you believe it…it's just something you have to know for yourself because girl, you take after my side of the family, and we tend to be some heavy women. Even so, and no matter what size you are or who is around you, you have to know that you're the best out of everyone. It's not about being cocky; it's about being sure of yourself."

The important lesson I learned from that moment and from the many others that followed was that it's up to me to love me. If I didn't understand and know that how God formed me from start to finish is unique to only me, I wouldn't be able to see what a treasure I really am.

Have you ever noticed that on days when you weren't necessarily trying to look divalicious for the masses and were just plain Jane, that people gave you the most beautiful compliments?

If so, then that experience has proven my point. When you embrace who you naturally are with all of your flaws, this gives people true insight to the real you, and you are wonderfully beautiful ladies. The magic behind this transaction is the person staring back at you receives the gift and freedom to love them self as well.

Assignments

Group

Take a look at your circle of girlfriends and write 3 beautiful features for each one. Call them up and let them know how their spirit helps you be a better woman, a better friend, a better mother, and lover of life. Be the leader for the people around you and encourage women to love the skin they're in.

Personal

Think of your skin as your favorite dress that glides on just right and hugs every curve. This dress is the essence of you and your sparkle and the base for an extraordinary ensemble. It's time to start building your perfect look. So go to your closet and pull out that special something that reminds you of your glow.

Deborah Harris

"Strength does not come from physical capacity. It comes from indomitable will."

—Mahatma Gandhi

Deborah Harris

CHAPTER TWO
I'm Every Woman

There's a clear reason why women are considered the best leaders throughout history. Women know how to get the job done. Period. Women take every experience from life and formal training in various arenas to produce an answer to unsolvable questions. I have come to believe that there is a mystical equation imbedded in the psyche of the female race that allows us to plug in up to 100 variables a day and come up with a favorable solution for every problem.

Women are also fierce contenders on every playing field because we think outside the box. Whether we are graduates from the school of hard knocks, an HBCU, or an Ivy League, the level of "Higher Learning" we've received has equipped us for every situation in life. On any given day, a singular woman will have the title of therapist, clean-up crew, doctor, lawyer, accountant, archeologist, site manager, and then some. Our genetic makeup gives us the ability to take what we learn and use it to our advantage in multiple scenarios. This type of woman does not limit herself to a box because she knows her value. It's like Whitney Houston said: "I'm every woman...it's all in me...anything you want done baby I do it naturally."

Not only are we geniuses when it comes to the system of life and making it bend to our will, women are chameleons. Having witty, innovative and strategically calculating character traits are accessories every lady tycoon should possess within her inner closet. One can think of it like having a loaded gun inside of your Birkin; classic, poised, clean and defined on the outside, yet fully capable of kicking tail and taking names on the inside.

Reflection

I typically get excited and have a sense of accomplishment these days when someone says that I'm a "Jack of all Trades." Funny thing is, I always thought I would be good at only one thing my whole life. For me, having multiple jobs seemed silly when I was younger because I was taught to stay focused and master one thing. I only wanted to focus on being really good at medicine since I was in the first grade. Every major paper I'd ever written in my younger years seemed to focus on me being an extraordinary doctor and helping people have longer and happier lives.

Well for me, life had other plans once college hit. My grades were horrific, and my focus was on at least 10 things at one time. I can't tell you how many different jobs and sectors I have worked in since graduating college. In retrospect, it has made me a better woman, aunt, lover, and citizen.

The bewildering thing that happened due to my various career moves (ups and downs), was that I couldn't really describe what it was I did per say or what I was good at. When I am asked these types of questions, I lead with a cheeky answer like "Whatever I choose to, and I'm good at everything."

At first, I was troubled with not believing I possessed a wide enough skill set to attain a job, but I was neglecting to see what I was good at and how many different ways I was able to shape my acquired skills to fit various needs. There is magic and value within all of us.

In many ways I like to think of the diversity of a woman in comparison with a shoe collection. On average, a lady's shoe collection contains sneakers, combat boots, booties with and without heels, stilettos, pumps, flats, and an array of sandals. On any given day, a woman must switch up her appearance and preparation for the next event. Anyone paying attention can tell where a woman is heading and about to accomplish based on her footwear.

Assignments

Group

Examine a collaborative shoe collection between yourself and your besties? What does the assortment say about you and your closest friends? Is there diversity among the group? Diversity is healthy within your circle of friends because you will constantly learn something new and gain new perspectives on life.

Personal

Are you sensible and calculating or tough and outgoing when it comes to your shoe collection? Take this opportunity to evaluate your eclectic personality and strengths and while you're at it, let's add the perfect footwear to the perfect dress you have picked out.

Deborah Harris

"Lasting change is a series of compromises. And compromise is all right, as long as your values don't change."

— Jane Goodall

Deborah Harris

CHAPTER THREE
Never Compromise

When most people think of compromising, they can sometimes have a negative connotation attached to losing something. This isn't always true and we have to be mindful of only looking at the meaning of compromise in this manner. However, for our purposes here when I say Never Compromise, I'm looking at it from a perspective of never giving up who you are at your core.

In other words, you can bend occasionally for those you love or to pose a solution to a problem but be mindful of when you begin shaving bits and pieces of one-self off in order to fit into someone else's mold.

Letting go of who you are in order to make someone else comfortable because you seem "too strong," "too charismatic," "too opinionated," "too caring," or "too bossy" is not a path you want to travel. As a people we must be aware that it takes time to get to know the heart of a person and the very characteristic that we perceive as "too much" is what makes an individual truly beautiful.

Far too often I hear stories from women of all ages who have at some point in their lives given up who they were in order to please someone else. In some instances this resulted in women never pursuing their dreams and never fully understanding who they were as an individual.

I've learned that in most circumstances when women are strong willed, it's because they have fought to have their will or personhood taken seriously. So often we are forced to fall in line with the crowd and not cause a stir, but if we remained silent and acceptant of the status quo then women such as Mother Theresa, Maya Angelou, and Susan B. Anthony would not have been able to offer up their voices and beliefs of change and retribution to the masses.

It's important that women see themselves as interchangeable beings that are capable of being soft and nurturing, while still personifying boldness that commands respect and honor. Having a mentality such as this allows you to be a person who can sympathize, empathize, and lend a helping hand while at the same time stand your ground with unwavering conviction.

Reflection

At the beginning of the year, I came upon a situation where I was faced with making money or telling the truth about the lack of accountability I saw taking place within an organization I was a partner in. This was a particularly difficult scenario because I went into the partnership believing that so many good things I wanted to bring into the community would be possible because of the people I partnered with.

For ten months I struggled, learned, and struggled some more until I realized that a final decision for my life and how I wanted to live it had to be made; it was time to look at the big picture and evaluate my stay with the company.

Whenever I went to work, I gave my all and made sacrifices and even placed myself in debt in order to see certain events and projects come together properly. Several months went by with me putting this company first before my own needs because I made promises to people on the outside and did not feel comfortable with disappointing others if I could help it. A few of my friends had noticed how stressed I had become and encouraged me to have faith in myself along with the accomplishments I made.

When the time came for me to part ways, the decision to walk away was one of the swiftest choices I've ever made in my life. Because I chose to walk away from the company and apologize to all those I had brought on board, many of my peers shamed me and were disappointed. While I knew it was the right thing to do, I knew that the choice would leave me in a state of abandonment and distanced from everything I helped to build.

I knew in this moment that I had grown to hold fast to my convictions because there was no doubt after the decision had been made, that I did what was best for me in the long run, and stood firm when so many voices thought I was crazy. This lesson taught me that you must have a firm grip on your foundation and beliefs about yourself and the way you would like the world to be. If we walk through life without a standard for excellence, we are privy to suffer many dark times without hope of redemption.

Assignment

Group

It's Bonfire time Ladies!! I love bonfires because they can go from quiet reflective moments to out right parties. Gather the girls and go around the fire speaking on your most vulnerable and courageous moments in life where you each stood up for yourself and stuck to your guns. Create a mantra of strength to repeat at the end of your gathering and toast to the strength of your collective voice.

Personal

Often times, we go through life not examining how far we've come. I urge you to take up a journal and write down moments where you didn't yield to the standards of others even when it seemed like the popular choice. I encourage this exercise because it helps you to see where your character and loyalty lies and how much you've grown. Always remember that it is acceptable to bend at times but never to break.

My mother used to say that a lady should always and with no excuse carry a purse. I'm sure you have a thousand choices to choose from in this area. So do your best to narrow your handbag down to just one. That outfit is coming together quite nicely don't you think?

"You owe it to yourself to live beautifully. And I am."

−Jill Scott

Deborah Harris

CHAPTER FOUR
Be at Peace, Full of Grace, and your Own Person

This chapter coincides with some pointers I gave in the Loving the Skin You're In segment. Remember that everything we learn is connected somehow and will come full circle in the end.

Living in peace, grace, and beauty comes when we are honest and loving toward ourselves first.

I truly believe with every fiber of my being that finding peace within oneself is one of the top five ultimate end goals of this life. Everything we experience shapes who we will be at the end of our time here on the Earth and how people will remember us. It is critical that you as a woman understand that the most important, beautiful, and life changing experiences you will have are the ones you have with yourself every day.

Learn how to be your own "Person" before you "Try" to be anyone else's.

If you are a fan of the popular television drama Grey's Anatomy, then you know what the phrase "My Person" means because of the friendship between Meredith and Christina. In short, Meredith and Christina were each other's life rafts because when one was drowning, the other was sticking out her hand as something to grab onto and hold on for dear life. Now while having key people in your corner to keep you going afloat and sane is all fine and dandy, we must be ready for the times in our lives when there will be no hand to grab or running the risk of pulling others down with us. We must all prepare ourselves for the seasons in our lives where we will be faced with letting go and feeling like we're in a desert place and no one is around for 1,000 miles.

As I look back on the many waste lands I've had to trudge through, I've come to the sobering fact that it was literally just me and God clawing my way to the light. There was no one with me during my late nights of experiencing insomnia and tears. There was no one in the passenger seat talking me out of driving my car off the freeway overpass. I couldn't speak to anyone about it really because I didn't want to place the negative and depressed energy off on anyone else to carry and quite frankly, I had a hard time putting how I felt into words and dealing with myself head on. During this stage, I had to be my own person. I had to say every dark, twisty, and miserable thing I was feeling out loud and then look at it from a non-emotional perspective: meaning deciphering between what's real and not real and the facts of the matter.

Its comes to my attention as I write this segment that many of you will not know how to even begin this journey and many of you will have an amazing testimony of how you have come out on the other side victoriously concerning this matter. I implore you to discover which sides of the coin you are dealing with at this moment in your life, because every interaction you have with the outside world is based upon how you interact with yourself before you allow anything or anyone else into your space. For example, if you wake up in the morning and your first thoughts are along the lines of "Woe is me," "Not Today," "I can't make it," or "I can't do this," then be prepared to have the universe throw that right back at you in various forms during the 12-16 hours that you're awake. When your foundational mindset is out of whack, you're not only harming yourself, but you're potentially harming everyone you come in contact with. How are you able to genuinely smile or encourage someone when you're dark and gloomy inside and don't have a strategy set in place to reroute your mood, emotions, or mentality so to speak? To answer the question quite honestly, everything you believe you're doing in these moments are only fragments of the amount of love you're trying to give because the love, grace, forgiveness, kindness, and understanding you have toward yourself is in pieces itself.

Once I was able to figure out a plan to reroute my mood and thinking, I could look myself in the mirror and decide what I wasn't going to let break me or define me. I chose truths that I wanted to believe and truths that were healthy for my self -esteem. I practiced speaking life and love and forgiveness over myself for as long as it took to feel the healing actually happening. After a few years, how I spoke to people and how they responded changed because I became my own life raft and realized that I'm worth saving.

I encourage women to take each year and moment that you are gifted with and be grateful and full of grace toward yourself and others. Many times it can be difficult to understand that the best gift we have to offer to ourselves and people around us is our love and understanding. It is true that we are our worst critiques and we are the hardest on ourselves. Often times we feel it silly or unnecessary to compliment ourselves on a job well done or even on our own beauty. There is a freedom and liberation with this exchange because it allows honesty and humility the opportunity to shine.

Often times we only see what people allow us to see and it generally revolves around the finished product or the pretty parts of their journey to success. It is a gift to have someone that is successful share his or her downfalls and shortcomings that they were faced with because we then begin to have a connection and care for them. We do not live for just ourselves in this life.

Whether we want to admit it or not, we will all leave an impact on someone.

It is an eye opening realization to know that people will not remember the fabulous brands you wore, the car you drove, or even the business you were president of. Material things do not equate to how beautiful of a life you've lived. Those that know of your name both near and far will recall your kindness, generosity, faithfulness, loyalty, convictions, and how you shaped a new generation of leaders. They will remember that you led a beautiful life.

Reflection

One of my favorite movies to date is *Eat Pray Love*. I was a little late with discovering this treasure but when I did, it opened me up to real beauty. I had fought so long to forget my hurts and failures. I tried to make my life look like the world's standard, and I became more lost than ever. I had no idea who I was and I lost sight of the importance of the journey. Because of this, I was filled with resentment and hatred toward the life I was living. I was alone within myself, and I could find no solitude. I thought at some points that God had abandoned me.

I ran toward every empty vice I could to fill the voids, but I had trouble connecting the dots. I soon realized that our stories and our journeys are different and specifically made for us and no one else. My arrival at the finish line can't be compared to someone else's crossing. Knowing this simple principal helped me embrace all of my broken pieces. I began to be grateful for the areas of my life and heart that were being healed. I was finally in a place where I could speak openly and honestly about my past and present, and it had a huge impact on my relationships with complete strangers. I'm not going to lie; some people distanced themselves and didn't quite understand my approach to many conflicts in life. What I enjoyed was the release of stress and tension in my life. I am able to walk with my head held high and encourage others to do the same.

It's like Julia Roberts' character said, "God lives in me as me." There is life in this statement and a gentleness that reminds us that we are perfect in our imperfections.

Assignment

Group

Don't you just love girl time? Well tonight is no different. So gather the ladies this Friday for a little mood board making. In the center of the board place a cutout of a mirror and at the top of the board place the phrase, "I am fearfully and wonderfully made." Gather up a few magazines and find words and letters that you can piece together that define who you want to be. When you are finished placing them on the board, go around in a circle and say them out loud while looking at yourself in the mirror. Smile and let your mind wrap itself around what's coming out of your mouth. Rejoice in the coming revival of your life.

Personal

Make a checklist of your supposed imperfections on one side of the paper. On the other side, list how each one has made you stronger and helped change your life for the better.

Every great outfit needs the perfect lady like accessories... earrings or necklace? Pearls it is!!! I'm a

Bosshion

pearl girl but by all means pick whatever you'd like girls.

Deborah Harris

"The question isn't who's going to let me; It is who's going to stop me."

-Ayn Rand

Deborah Harris

CHAPTER FIVE
You Too Can Move Mountains

It is encouraging to see so many people accomplishing great things in this lifetime. Questions concerning the right formula for greatness are being posed day after day in various circles. The irony about the greatness formula is that it doesn't equal an exact answer nor require any tangible specifics: greatness can follow anyone from any walk of life. The one thing I'd say that great leaders have in common is that they walked to the beat of their own drum. Walking to the beat of your own drum creates magic. Magic isn't necessarily based on a specific amazing thing happening, but it's more about freeing oneself and gracing others with that freedom. We shouldn't create a standard of whether or not you're required to have a college degree, street smarts, a trust fund, or two pennies to your name in order to qualify for greatness. Anyone can attain greatness at any level in life.

Ladies, remember that you can move mountains. Your mountain may not look like the next person's, but it is your mountain to climb and conquer. Remember that you have been equipped for a time such as this, and everything you have gathered along the way is a tool to chip away at that obstacle in front of you. Your voice and your heart matters, and you are amazing and a roaring lion. Be a leader where God has placed you. Be a trendsetter and set the pace for other women and young ladies looking up to you. Encourage them to write their own stories and formula to being a Boss in their lives.

Reflection

I was blessed enough to have great and mighty

women in my life when I needed so much guidance and assurance that I was worthy of love and happiness. All of my mentors in college were bold and fearless and kept me in check concerning being truthful with what I really wanted and how to go after it. They taught me balance and self-love. They had high standards and were so hard on me because I used to give up on myself too easily. When I look at these women now and all the many things they have accomplished, I am in awe and even more determined to move my own mountain. These women have built beautiful homes, raised children, and went after masters' degrees while building successful blogs and writing songs, to being great teachers and community leaders, and small business owners. Their hunger and determination is contagious, and it drives me to push even harder for what I believe will make a difference in this world and in so many lives.

Remember that you have a right to desire greatness from yourself. Do not turn away from your mountain at the first sight of trouble. If need be, gather some friends and loved ones who can lend you a tool or two to chip away at what's blocking you from becoming a leader in your own life.

Assignment

Group

Your perfect outfit is ready and most importantly, so are you! You've examined yourself from within and you're ready to walk into a new chapter, looking and feeling more radiant than ever. Plan a tea or dinner with the courageous women you've journeyed with during this process, and go over the purpose behind ever stunning outfit you see in the room. You will be amazed at how meaningful and expressive clothes are and now you will know more about the deepest treasures behind them.

Personal

Make a list of your hills and mountains and a game plan to remove them all. Place it where you can see it every day and as you begin to remove pieces of the mountain, write it down and rejoice in your victories no matter how small.

CLOSING NOTE

I heard something the other day from a movie that opened my eyes to the joy of being alive and being able to choose how I want to be remembered. The character said, "It is the people that no one imagines anything of, that do the things that no one imagines."

Take a good hard look in the mirror because you are staring at someone that will change lives and break boundaries. You are staring at the future and hope. You are staring at the Earth and every good thing that springs from it. Take the world by storm and cause a little trouble.

BE A BOSS!

Sincerely,

Your sister in arms

Deborah Harris

Deborah Harris

Deborah Harris

www.ingramcontent.com/pod-product-compliance
Lightning Source LLC
Chambersburg PA
CBHW071429040426
42445CB00012BA/1320